PAUL S. SCHUDER
Science Collections

Woodland Public Library

Mimbres design from Art of a Vanished Race

Dead Log Alive!

Dead Log Alive!

by Jo S. Kittinger

A FIRST BOOK

FRANKLIN WATTS
A DIVISION OF GROLIER PUBLISHING

NEW YORK   LONDON   HONG KONG   SYDNEY
DANBURY, CONNECTICUT

Photo credits ©: Helen H. Kittinger: p. 21; Jo S. Kittinger: pp. 8, 10, 26, 37: Photo Researchers: cover, pp. 2, 29 (all photos Tom & Pat Lesson), 16 (Nick Bergkessel), 20 (Scott Camazine), 34 (Stephen Maslowski), 40 (Peter Katsaros), 41 (Tom McHugh), 42 (J.H. Robinson), 43 (Phil A. Dotson), 46 (Larry West), 49 (Harold Hungerford), 52 (Gilbert Grant), 53 (William H. Mullins); Visuals Unlimited: pp. 14 (Valerie Hodgson), 18 (Maslowski Photo), 22 (McCutheon), 24 (Sylvia Duran Sharnoff), 25 (Stanley Flegler), 31 (Tom J. Ulrich), 32 (S. Maslowski), 39 (J. Alcock), 48 (Ken Lucas), 51, 55 (both photos Doug Sokell).

Author photo ©: Helen H. Kittinger

Library of Congress Cataloging-in-Publication Data

Jo S. Kittinger.
    Dead Log Alive! / by Jo S. Kittinger.
       p. cm. — (A First book)
    Includes bibliographical references and index.
Summary: Describes the variety of animal and plant life found on, in, and around dead logs, and explains the role that dying trees play in nature's cycles.
    ISBN 0-531-20237-2
    1. Forest ecology—Juvenile literature. 2. Forest animals—Habitat—Juvenile literature. 3. Trees—Ecology—Juvenile literature.
    I. Title. II. Series.
    QH541.5.F6K57 1996
    574.5'2642—dc20   96-11624 CIP AC

Contents

Dead Log Alive!

Home Is a Snag

*L*ightning strikes! A tree is dead. You might think it is a terrible loss when a fine old tree dies. But this isn't the end of the tree's usefulness. It is the beginning of a new phase in the life cycle.

Trees die from a variety of causes. The weather can be a killer. Lightning, strong winds, tornadoes, or hurricanes kill some trees. Ice that builds up can be so heavy that the branches snap. Too much rain (and the floods that can result) or too little rain can kill trees.

Tiny insects can bore into giant trees, causing damage to the wood and making the tree vulnerable to disease. Bigger animals, such as beavers, also take a toll. And a variety of human activities can kill trees. (Have you heard the story of George Washington and the cherry tree?)

A dead tree that is still standing is called a snag. These barren tree trunks, stripped of their leaves and limbs, and all the logs scattered across the forest floor, have special places in the cycle of life.

What good can come of a dead tree? More than you might imagine. This book will cover a few of the thousands of plants and animals in North America that use a dead tree for food

This snag has a nest that was carved out by a woodpecker.

or shelter. Some are quite large, others so small you would need a microscope to see them. Some animals use a dead tree while it is still standing. Fungi grow on the surface. Insects bore right into the wood for food or shelter. If a log is hollow, animals might use it as a den. Underneath a dead log you can discover all kinds of living things. (But be careful—some of them are dangerous.)

Finally, though we cannot see microscopic organisms, we can certainly see the effect of their work on the log. Bacteria, for example, break wood down into compounds that enrich the soil, enabling more trees to grow. This completes the life cycle. Not all of the plants and animals in this book can be found in all parts of North America. But you can be sure that similar things are living in a dead log near you.

From large to small, from the outside in—you will see that a dead log is still very much alive—with other living things.

Chapter One

Flying In

One of the first things you'll notice about a snag or fallen log is that it's full of holes. Where did they come from? Many small holes are made by insects. But the larger holes, the ones you'll see first, are usually made by woodpeckers.

There are more than twenty *species* (types) of woodpeckers in North America. Most of them are *cavity* nesting birds, meaning they make nests in hollow places. Dead limbs or dead trees are the first choice for most woodpeckers looking to build a home.

Woodpeckers see a snag as both an apartment and a cafeteria, finding shelter and food there. It seems as if it would hurt to bang your head against a tree. But woodpeckers are equipped with strong neck muscles and a long bill like a chisel. Muscles on the head act as shock absorbers. It is natural for woodpeckers to drill holes, because they are "designed" to do it.

Nesting cavities are usually made high in the tree, about 30 to 60 feet (9 to 18 m) above ground. The opening is just big enough for the woodpecker. Inside, the cavity is 6 to 25 inches (15 to 63 cm) deep. It can take up to a month for a pair of woodpeckers to hollow out the place they have selected. A few wood chips are all they use to line the nest.

A powerful bill allows woodpeckers to excavate nesting holes and probe tree bark for food. But woodpeckers have other features that are useful for their way of life, too. They use their stiff tail feathers to brace against the tree as they are pounding away. And unlike other birds, most woodpeckers have two front toes and two back toes to help them hold on while they work. But perhaps the most interesting special feature is the woodpecker's tongue.

A woodpecker's tongue can extend to great lengths— up to three times the length of the bill! The tongue is attached to a structure of bone and elastic tissue called the hyoid. This *hyoid structure* wraps around the skull and pushes the tongue out when the bird is feeding. The tongue is also covered with a sticky substance and is sometimes barbed, like the end of a fishing hook. Insects and their *larvae* that have burrowed into a tree have little defense against such a weapon. Because the wood-boring insects that woodpeckers eat are available throughout the year, few woodpeckers migrate.

At 16 to 19 inches (41 to 48 cm) long, the pileated woodpecker (*Dryocopus pileatus*) is the largest woodpecker commonly found in America. The Latin word *dryas* means "tree" and *copis* means "cleaver" or "chopper." *Pileus* means cap, so this bird's name means capped tree chopper. A male

Pileated Woodpecker

pileated woodpecker can be distinguished from a female by the red "mustache" he wears. The call of a male pileated woodpecker is a loud "**Kak Kak Kak Kak,**" like something from a jungle movie.

One species of woodpecker is even larger. The ivory-billed woodpeckers (*Campephilus principalis*) can be 20 inches (51 cm) long. They look very much like the pileated. They are almost *extinct*, however. For many years it was assumed they had all died. Now it is believed that a few pairs remain in western Cuba.

The red-headed woodpecker (*Melanerpes erythro-cephalus*) is one of the easiest to identify. With its solid red head and stark black-and-white body, you will not confuse it with any other bird. Both sexes are identical in appearance. Its call is a raucous "**Kwrrk.**"

A pair of woodpeckers will often use several tree cavities in a single season, one for nesting and others for roosting spots, since the pair do not sleep together. The male and female share many responsibilities; the male even sits on eggs. At times *predators*, such as snakes or aggressive birds, like starlings, will force the woodpeckers to move from one nesting hole to another. Unfortunately, there is often a shortage of suitable snags. People often remove dead trees, assuming this will cut down on disease and make room for healthy trees. Foresters are now seeing, however, that these dead trees are vital to cavity nesting birds. In turn, these birds are needed to help keep the forest insect population under control.

Southern Flying Squirrel

When woodpeckers move out, others move in. A variety of birds use vacant woodpecker holes as nesting sites. They are called *secondary* residents. These include bluebirds, nuthatches, screech owls, and chickadees. Woodpeckers lay solid white eggs, so if you find colored or speckled eggs in a woodpecker hole, you can be sure they were laid by a secondary resident.

Mammals also make their home in woodpecker cavities, sometimes enlarging them in the process. Mice, squirrels, and raccoons can all be found living in snags. Deserted woodpecker holes are the favorite nesting sites of flying squirrels, although these and other mammals will nest in any suitable hole.

The southern flying squirrel *(Glaucomys volans)* and the northern flying squirrel *(Glaucomys sabrinus)* are very similar in appearance, although the northern species is larger. Both have very soft, silky fur and large black eyes.

Flying squirrels do not actually fly. That is, they do not power themselves through the air, but they do glide through it. A loose fold of skin, stretching along each side from wrist to ankle, acts as a combination parachute and sail. A wide, furry, flat tail helps guide its flight. "Flights" of more than 150 feet (46 meters) from one tree trunk to another have been observed.

Flying squirrels are *nocturnal* creatures, meaning they hunt for food only at night. They are *omnivores*, which means they eat both plants and meat. They love nuts, berries, acorns, seeds, insects, and birds' eggs.

During extremely cold weather, several flying squirrels may den together for warmth. Since they are nocturnal, it is difficult to spot one of these beautiful brown animals. However, if you scrape a snag that has a woodpecker hole, you may be lucky enough to awaken a flying squirrel who will poke its head out to investigate the noise.

\/\/\/\/\

Flying Squirrel sitting on Bracket Fungus

Chapter Two

Living on the Outside

According to *mycologists* (people who study fungi), there are more than 100,000 species of fungi. In the past, fungi were thought of as nongreen plants because they have no *chlorophyll* (the green substance that plants use to convert sunlight into food). But fungi have no leaves or roots either. They take in food more like animals. Actually they are not plants or animals—they are regarded as belonging to a separate kingdom in the classification of living things. Fungi living on dead logs are *saprophytes*, meaning they are able to get their food from the dead material they grow on.

Fungi live all around us in the soil, water, and air. Most are too small to be seen. Even the fungi we can see have already been around long before anyone notices. That's because thousands of threadlike cells, called *hyphae*, start to grow under the surface of the material on which the fungus feeds. These tiny branching cells form a tangled mass, the *mycelium*.

When conditions such as temperature and moisture are just right for the fungus, the fruiting body (which we call a mushroom) grows very quickly. You might wake up one morning to find your yard full of mushrooms that weren't there the day before. They disappear just as quickly, when they have produced *spores*. These are scattered by wind and water. A spore that finds a suitable place soon begins to produce a new fungus.

Orange Mycena Mushrooms

Fungi have many forms—from single-celled fungi, to some that look like soft coral, to giant toadstools more than 1 foot (30 cm) across. Two types that often live on decaying logs are mushrooms of the *Mycena* genus and *brackets* of the *Trametes* genus.

The *Mycena* mushrooms have small caps and long, thin stems. They often grow in large groups on decaying hardwood. Their spores are produced within gills underneath the cap.

Turkey Tail Fungus

The brackets of the *Trametes* genus grow like shelves on a dead tree or log. One species is appropriately named "turkey tails." It has rings of brown and tan with a ruffled edge. The turkey tail brackets are leathery and form large overlapping tiered groups. These fungi do not have gills. The spores are produced in tubes and come out through pores. Unlike most mushrooms, which have a short life span, the brackets of these fungi can live more than a year.

Moss covers the ground in this Alaska forest.

You will find moss growing on dead logs, too. Mosses also grow on the ground and even on rocks. Like mushrooms, they do not have true roots. They have threadlike structures called *rhizoids* that resemble roots. The rhizoids anchor the plant to the surface on which it grows (the *substratum*). A short stem grows from the rhizoids and is covered with tiny leaves that spiral around the stem.

Unlike mushrooms, mosses contain chlorophyll and make their own food by using sunlight (this process is called *photosynthesis*). Mosses are always some shade of green. Some plants, such as Spanish moss or reindeer moss, have the word moss in their name, but they are not really mosses. Reindeer moss is really a lichen, and Spanish moss is actually in the pineapple family! There are over 9,000 species of mosses. More than 1,200 grow in North America. It takes a lot of study to identify the individual species.

During dry periods, mosses may turn dull brown and look dead. They are said to be "crisped" in this state. As soon as it rains, however, they become green and fresh-looking again. Mosses are not dependent on roots. Water is absorbed through all parts of the plant. This lets them revive quickly in the rain. Scientists have tested mosses and found that some can revive after being without water for as long as ten years!

Mosses tend to grow in bunches. You may have seen and felt a thick moss mat in the woods. These mats, made up of thousands of moss plants, can grow to cover an entire log.

A Foliose Lichen on the bark of a tree

Mosses and fungi are not the only things you might find living on a dead log. You will certainly see lichens, maybe you'll see resurrection fern, and if you're really lucky you will find a good, healthy slime mold, too!

A lichen is an organism that consists of an alga and a fungus living together as a single unit. The alga is a plant-like organism that has chlorophyll but does not have a vascular system to transport food and materials around in its body. It makes food with chlorophyll and sunlight. The fungus cannot make food, but it absorbs water quickly, which moves materials around. There are about 20,000 species of lichens, and they fall into three groups. Fruiticose lichens attach to the bark (or other substratum) only at the base, so that it has a shrublike appearance. Foliose lichens resemble tiny leaves, often in a whirl. Crustose lichens are crust-like in appearance and have their entire undersurface attached to the log. You can easily find examples of all three lichen groups on dead trees and logs.

Slime molds are amazing. Sometimes they are classified as plants and other times they are classified as animals! In one respect, it resembles an animal. The jellylike mass,

Red Slime Mold

Resurrection Fern growing with moss and a Turkey Tail Fungus on a dead log

called a *plasmodium*, has the power of slow creeping movement. Like fungi, mosses, and some other plants, though, slime molds reproduce by spores. They are often white, orange, or red and can grow to be 1 foot (30 cm) across.

Resurrection fern *(Polypodium polypodioides)* is a small fern that you can find growing on either living or dead trees. Even though it grows on another plant, this fern is not a parasite. It produces its own food. Resurrection fern was appropriately named. During dry spells it shrivels up and looks dead. It quickly revives in the rain, though, appearing to come back to life.

Chapter   Three

The Family Room

Have you ever heard this riddle? "If a tree falls in the forest and there is no one there to hear it, does it make a noise?"

Well, maybe no humans are there to hear the noise, but there are all kinds of animals in the forest that hear it, and if they like what's left of the tree, they call it home.

Large trees that have died are sometimes hollow, the center having rotted out over time. When they fall, the hollow logs offer temporary shelter from rain and cold to all the forest animals. There are two mammals in particular that often choose a hollow log as the place to make their den and give birth to their young. These two animals are the North American porcupine and the gray fox.

The North American porcupine *(Erothizon dorsatum)* is sometimes called the tree porcupine or the Canadian porcupine. It lives in Canada and most of the United States, except the southeast. The female porcupine will enter her

This Porcupette (left) was well developed at birth, but it will remain with the adult Porcupine (right) for many months.

log home in the spring and give birth to a single cub, or "porcupette," after a pregnancy of about seven months. This is a long *gestation period* for a small animal, so the porcupette is very well developed at birth. Its eyes are open, and it is covered with long black fur and soft wet *quills*. The quills begin to harden as they dry. The porcupette begins to eat solid food within two weeks but continues to take milk from its mother for up to four months. Baby porcupines can begin to climb small trees when they are only a few days old!

Adult porcupines are usually 3 to 3½ feet long (91 to 107 cm) and 15 to 20 pounds (7 to 9 kg). However, some large males have weighed in at 40 pounds (18 kg). They are good climbers and spend much of their time in trees, looking for food or resting. Porcupines are *herbivores*, meaning they only eat plants. In the summer they eat a variety of plants, but in winter they live mainly on tree bark.

Porcupines are nocturnal (active at night), so it is uncommon to find one. If you do happen to see one in the woods, do not be afraid. Porcupines will not attack their enemies, nor can they shoot their quills through the air, as some people think.

When the porcupine is relaxed, the quills lie down and are almost hidden by a coat of long brown guard hairs. If you alarm the porcupine, it will turn its back to you and raise its quills in defense. If you come too close, it will begin striking with its tail. The thousands of quills are loosely

**Porcupines chew things to keep their teeth sharp.
This one has found a deer antler in the snow.**

attached. They come out easily and stick into the flesh of attackers. Porcupine quills are long sharp bristles of hair that have grown together. There are many sharp barbs, like the tips of a fishing hook. These barbs cause the quills to work their way into the flesh; this makes them difficult to remove. But remember, the porcupine will not bother you unless you bother it.

The porcupine is a rodent (a gnawing animal), like rats, mice, hamsters, and beavers. They have four long yellow

The Gray Fox climbs trees to escape danger and to find food.

teeth, called *incisors*, that continually grow. To keep them sharp and ground down they have to keep chewing.

Many people consider porcupines pests. Sometimes porcupines eat a complete ring of bark from around a tree and the tree dies. They also crave salt. To satisfy this taste, they will gnaw tool handles and oars that have been held in sweaty hands, as well as gloves, boots, and saddles.

The gray fox *(Urocyon cinereoargenteus)* is unique among the North American foxes. It is sometimes called a tree fox because it can actually climb trees! Sometimes other foxes, like the red fox, may run up a leaning tree to outfox an enemy, but the gray fox can climb catlike up a straight tree. It cannot run as fast or as far as other species of foxes, so it usually climbs to escape danger.

The gray fox climbs not only when pursued but also to get food. It loves wild cherries, grapes, and birds' eggs. Despite their fondness for fruit, foxes are considered *carnivores* because they mainly eat meat. They hunt for mice, squirrels, birds, and insects. They also scavenge for scraps left by other animals or put in the garbage.

The gray fox is easy to recognize. Its coat is a grizzled gray, and it has a long bushy tail. A black stripe runs down its back and tail. The fur around the ears, neck, legs, and sides is often rusty red and the belly is white. Gray foxes are fairly small, about 6 to 15 pounds (3 to 7 kg) and about 30 inches (76 cm) long, not counting the tail.

Young fox cubs need to be protected for at least five months. A hollow in a dead log provides the perfect den.

Most other fox species build dens in underground burrows. The gray fox, however, prefers to den in hollow logs, in caves, or among rocks. The female fox, called a *vixen*, gives birth in the spring after a two-month gestation period. The average litter has three or four cubs but can range from one to seven.

Unlike baby porcupines, gray fox cubs are blind and helpless at birth. They drink their mother's milk for six weeks before being ready for solid food. The male fox, called a dog, remains with the mother and cubs in the hollow log, helping protect and feed the young. When they are about five months old the cubs leave the parents.

Even though gray foxes live in most of the United States, and also in parts of Canada, Mexico, and Central America, most people will never see one. In addition to being nocturnal, they are shy and are good at keeping out of sight. If you find a hollow log in the woods, look around for evidence, like fur or chewed bones. Perhaps a fox used it as a den.

C h a p t e r   F o u r

Beware What's Under There

If you've ever rolled over a rotting log, you've probably seen a variety of creatures scurry in all directions. The habitat under the log is perfect for many animals that seek protection and food. Most are harmless, but animals that bite or sting often hide beneath a log, so always be careful when looking there.

Snakes are among the earth's most feared creatures. Many of our fears are based on myths and superstitions. Actually, of the 115 species of snakes found north of Mexico, only 17 species are *venomous* (poisonous). However, you do need to be cautious around all snakes. Many can give you a painful bite even if they aren't venomous. But snakes usually bite only when they feel threatened. They will not go out of their way to attack you.

If you know a snake is *not* poisonous and you wish to pick it up, be careful to protect both yourself and the snake. *(If you don't know whether it's poisonous, don't pick it up!)* If it is big, wear thick leather gloves. Use a forked stick to hold the snake in place while you pick it up. You need to place the fork of the stick directly behind the snake's head. Grasp the snake behind its head with one hand and support its body with your other hand.

One snake often found under rotting logs is the gentle ringneck snake *(Diadophis punctatus)*. Other common names for this species are ring snake or collared snake.

The ringneck snake is *nonvenomous* and rarely bites. It is slender and has smooth scales. Its color varies from brown to black. You will see right away how it got its name. There

Ringneck Snake near its nest in a rotting log

is a distinctive yellow or orange ring around the neck. The underside of the ringneck snake varies from bright yellow to reddish-orange.

All snakes are exclusively carnivorous, and they swallow their prey whole. The ringneck snake eats salamanders, lizards, insect larvae, young snakes, frogs, and worms. What better place to look for this menu than under a fallen tree?

The ringneck snake also uses the rotting log as its nesting site. Some snakes bear live young and some lay eggs. The ringneck snake is *oviparous*—an egg layer. The females usually lay their slender whitish eggs in rotting wood within a log or stump. The rotting process going on in fallen trees actually generates some heat, which helps to incubate the eggs. Moisture, trapped in the loose wood, helps to keep the eggs from drying out.

The nest usually contains four or five eggs in a *clutch*. Some larger clutches have been found, and *herpetologists* (scientists who study reptiles and amphibians) suppose that more than one ringneck snake may sometimes use the same nest. Indeed, these snakes are *gregarious*, which means they often huddle together in secretive places.

Another feared creature is the scorpion. Scorpions are known for their lobsterlike pincers and their long curved tail that ends with a poisonous stinger. Scorpions are in the Arachnida class along with spiders. Arachnids differ from insects because they don't have wings or antennae, and they have eight legs instead of six.

There are more than seventy species of scorpions in North America. While they are most common in the southern states, scorpions have been found as far north as Alberta, Canada. All scorpions are venomous and can inflict a sting that may cause painful swelling. Only two species, however—

Female Scorpion carrying her young on her back

Centruroides sculpturatus (known as the bark scorpion, or slender or sculptured scorpion) and *Centruroides gertschi*—are considered to have a potentially deadly sting. Both types are found in the southwestern United States.

Female scorpions are *viviparous*, meaning they give birth to live young. You might be lucky enough to see a female scorpion carrying her large brood of babies on her back. She will carry them with her for two to three weeks.

Scorpions are some of the hardiest animals you will find. They normally eat spiders and soft-bodied insects. They can live a long time with very little food or water and can survive extreme temperatures. They can even survive after being frozen in ice or being under water for days.

If under the log you find a creature that seems to be all legs, it is either a centipede or a millipede. You should know, though, that millipedes and centipedes are very different animals.

Millipedes, which belong to the class Diploda, are herbivorous. They eat only plants and are harmless. Centipedes, on the other hand, belong to the class Chilipoda and are carnivorous. They feed on insect larvae, slugs, snails, and worms. Some larger species can inflict a painful bite.

You can easily tell them apart. Millipedes move slowly. They have rounded body segments, each with two pairs of legs. Centipedes move quickly in order to catch their prey. They have only one pair of legs on each segment, and the segments are flattened.

Millipedes and centipedes sometimes look similar. The easiest
way to tell them apart is by the number of legs per section:
a millipede (left) has two pairs of legs per section;
a centipede (above) has one pair per section.

The Pill Bug, or "roly poly," can roll itself up into a tight ball when it senses danger.

Have you ever found a "roly poly" under a log or stone? When you pick one up, it quickly rolls into a tight ball. But if you stay very still, it will uncurl and walk around on your hand. Don't worry—it's harmless.

There are two animals in the United States commonly called roly poly—the pill millipede (*Glomeris romana* is one common species) and a wood louse called the pill bug *(Armadillidium vulgare)*. Some people refer to roly polies as sow bugs. Sow bugs are another wood louse and look similar, but most of them cannot roll into a tight ball. You can tell the difference between pill millipedes and pill bugs by the number of legs. Pill bugs have seven pairs of legs. Pill millipedes, of which there are various species, always have more than seven pairs of legs.

Roll over a log near water and you might discover a slimy, wet salamander. About one hundred species of salamanders live in the United States and Canada. There are perhaps five hundred different species worldwide. They are all amphibians (from the class Amphibia), which generally means starting life with gills and living in water but then becoming air-breathing adults capable of coming onto land. Some salamanders follow this pattern, having both *aquatic* and land life stages. Some salamanders, however, spend their entire lives in water and others live and breed entirely on land.

Many species of salamanders might be found under a dead tree. The key is to look in damp areas. One of the most common is the slimy salamander *(Plethodon glutinous)*, also called the sticky salamander. It can secrete a substance from

Slimy Salamander

43

its skin glands that is very difficult to wash off your hands. This goo is harmless to people, but it may be toxic to some predators, such as frogs.

The slimy salamander is rather large—up to 8 inches (20.5 cm) long. It is black with silvery white spots or brassy flecks. It can be found in most of the eastern United States. This salamander likes to lay its eggs in well-rotted logs, skipping the aquatic phase that most salamanders go through. The slimy salamander is nocturnal and carnivorous. It hunts at night for worms, insects, and other small creatures.

The underside of a dead log is perhaps the best spot to look for a wide variety of animals. In addition to these salamanders, roly polies, scorpions, and snakes, a host of other animals will slither, slide, and burrow to escape when you turn over a log. Field guides on insects, reptiles, amphibians, and arachnids can help you identify them.

It is important to remember safety when disturbing animals in their natural habitat. Wear heavy shoes or boots in areas where poisonous snakes live. When you approach a fallen tree, do not stick your hand or unprotected foot under the log. Kick or roll the log over as you watch carefully for what is underneath. Step back as the log rolls, in case you uncover a snake. Remember that venomous animals are to be respected but not feared. And be considerate when you leave. Roll the log back to its original location for those who call it home.

Chapter Five

Insect City

While you're investigating your log, knock to see if anyone is home. After you knock, press your ear to the wood. If you hear a distinct rustling sound, there may be an active *colony* of carpenter ants. They make this sound with mouthparts called *mandibles*, but it is not from the chewing of wood. Instead, it might be a form of communication.

If you hear a ticking sound, you may have disturbed a colony of termites. Soldier termites produce this sound when alarmed. Both termites and carpenter ants build elaborate "cities" with many tunnels and chambers in the dead wood. They are both insects (having three body parts—head, abdomen and thorax—six legs, and antennae) and both are called "social" insects.

Like honeybees, thousands of ants or termites live and work together in a colony. The colony consists of large numbers of workers and soldiers, a few kings (reproductive males), and one or more queens (reproductive females) who lay all the eggs. These separate groups are called *castes*. Each caste has a different body type suitable for its job. You may see some ants or termites with wings. These are the new reproductive males and females who will soon leave the nest. They will fly away, then lose their wings, mate, and perhaps start a new colony.

Sometimes people call termites white ants, but they are more closely related to roaches than to ants. In fact, termites and ants are different in many ways. Termites are usu-

It is easy to see all the basic body parts of a carpenter ant—head, abdomen, thorax, legs, and antennae.

ally pale in color and have no eyes, whereas carpenter ants are generally black and have well-developed eyes. Ants have a thin "waist" and termites do not. The wings of the reproductive termites have two pairs of very long wings that are both the same length. New reproductive ants have two pairs of wings, but the forewings are longer than the hindwings.

Their life cycles are also different. Termites hatch from their eggs as *nymphs*. They look similar to the adults and take an active part in the work of the colony before they are fully grown. Carpenter ants emerge from eggs as larvae, which are helpless and must be fed by the workers. The larvae then *pupate* inside silken pupal cases where they transform into adult ants.

Although ants and termites both make *galleries* (tunnels) in dead wood, they do it for different reasons. Termites actually eat the wood. They have microscopic protozoa in their intestines that enable them to break down the cellulose of the wood so they can digest it. Usually their nest is in the ground beneath the log.

Carpenter ants do not eat the wood. The log itself, with its tunnels, is their home. They eat insects, fruit juices, and *honeydew* (a sweet liquid given off by tiny insects called aphids). Many carpenter ants keep aphids in a "corral" on a plant where they protect them from predators. Then, at regular intervals, the ants "milk" the aphids; that is, they stroke the aphids, which makes them release the honeydew.

Both termites and carpenter ants carve galleries, or tunnels, into dead wood. Termite galleries are rough in appearance, because the termites actually eat the wood; they keep their nests below the log in the ground.

Carpenter ant galleries appear cleaner; they live in these tunnels.

If someone helps you to break open the rotten log, you can see the galleries. Even if there are no insects present, you may be able to determine which insect made the tunnels. Carpenter ant galleries are very clean and smooth, looking almost as if they've been sandpapered. (That's how they got the name carpenter ants.) Termite tunnels will not be as clean and will have a rougher appearance.

If you find narrow tunnel-like patterns between the bark and trunk of a dead tree, you've probably discovered the work of bark beetles. There are various species of these small insects that are generally less than ¼ inch (6 cm) long. They spend most of their lives inside the tree. Only in early summer do the adults emerge and fly to new trees.

Other more impressive beetles also use rotten logs for nesting. The patent leather beetle, bessbug, or horned passalus *(Odontotaenius disjunctus)*, all names for the same insect, is 1⅛ to 1⅜ inches (30 to 35 mm) long and has parallel grooves on its back. When disturbed, patent leather beetles make a squeaking sound by rubbing roughened areas under their wings across their backs. These sounds are called *stridulations*. Other insects, such as crickets, make similar sounds with their wings or legs. But each species' sound is unique.

Adult patent leather beetles eat decaying wood, and they prechew the food for larvae. They lay eggs in galleries that other adult beetles and larvae have excavated.

This dramatic pattern in the wood beneath the bark of
a dead tree is a series of tunnels dug by Bark Beetles.

Elephant Stag Beetle

The largest beetle you are likely to find under a log is the reddish-brown elephant stag beetle, also called the giant stag beetle *(Lucanus elephus)*, which can be up to 2 inches (5 cm) long. (The largest beetle in the world, the long-horned beetle, is sometimes 8 inches [20 cm] long!) The elephant stag beetle looks fierce with its extremely large, pronged mandibles, which look like antlers. The female of the species has much smaller mandibles than the male. The pinching bug *(Pseudolucanus capreolus)* is a similar stag beetle that grows up to 1½ inches long (38 mm). While you might be afraid to touch these impressive insects, they are capable of only a mild pinch.

Adult stag beetles lay their eggs in rotting wood. When the eggs hatch, the larvae feed on the decaying wood around them. Beetle larvae look like white worms in the log. Some people call these "grubs."

From the holes made by woodpeckers to the chewing of the termites, many living things help break down the wood of a dead tree and return it to the soil. This process

In old-growth forests like Mount Hood National Forest in Oregon, dead trees decompose and enrich the soil to encourage the growth of other trees and plants.

is called *decomposition*. Without decomposition all life would eventually stop. Dead trees and animals would forever remain where they fell. The elements needed for new life would stay locked inside them.

Bacteria are essential to decomposition. These one-celled organisms live all around us. Many are saprophytes and live on dead plants and animals. While fulfilling their own needs they break down the wood of a log into its basic elements. These elements become part of the soil and are absorbed and used by plants. Plants in turn produce oxygen and food for animals and people. Even when dead, trees play an important part in the cycle of life.

Dead leaves and new growth cover the forest floor, until old dead wood becomes almost impossible to see.

Glossary

Aquatic — growing or living in water.

Bracket — a leathery, shelflike structure that is the fruiting body of certain fungi.

Carnivore — an animal that eats meat (adj. carnivorous).

Caste — distinct group within a species.

Cavity — a hollow place.

Chlorophyll — the green substance that enables a green plant to make its own food by harnessing the sun's light energy.

Clutch — a group of eggs.

Colony — a group of insects that live and work together.

Decomposition — the process in which organic material is broken down into its basic elements and is returned to the soil.

Extinct — members of a particular species are no longer alive.

Galleries — tunnels made in wood by insects.

Gestation period — the length of time an animal is pregnant.

Gregarious — tends to gather in groups.

Herbivore — an animal that eats plants (adj. herbivorous).

Herpetologist — a scientist who studies reptiles and amphibians.

Honeydew — a sugary liquid produced by certain insects.

Hyoid structure — bone and elastic tissue that enables a woodpecker to extend its tongue unusually far.

Hyphae — threadlike cells that make up the main part of a fungus.

Incisors — the front cutting teeth of an animal.

Larva (plural "larvae") — the immature wormlike form of an insect.

Mandibles — a pair of jaws on an insect that move from side to side.

Mycelium — a tangled mass of hyphae, which is part of a fungus.

Mycologist — a scientist who studies fungi.

Nocturnal — active at night.

Nonvenomous — not poisonous.

Nymph — a young insect that resembles the adult form but has not yet reached maturity.

Omnivore — an animal that eats both meat and plants (adj. omnivorous).

Oviparous — lays eggs.

Photosynthesis — the process by which a green plant makes its own food.

Plasmodium — the jellylike mass of a slime mold.

Predator — an animal that hunts other animals for food.

Pupate — to pass through a stage in insect life from larva to adult insect.

Quills — long, sharp, thick bristles of hair on a porcupine.

Rhizoids — the rootlike structures of mosses.

Saprophyte — an organism that lives off dead or decaying organic matter.

Secondary — second in order.

Snag — a standing dead tree that has lost most of its branches.

Species — a class of living things having common characteristics.

Spores — tiny reproductive structures produced by fungi, mosses, and ferns that are able to grow into a new plant.

Stridulations — noise made by an insect rubbing body parts together.

Substratum — the surface on which a moss or fungus grows.

Venomous — poisonous.

Viviparous — gives birth to live young.

Vixen — a female fox.

For Further Reading

Behnke, Francis L. *A Natural History of Termites.* New York: Charles Scribner's Sons, 1977.

Buxton, Ralph. *Nature's Gliders—The Flying Squirrels.* Chicago: Children's Press, 1975.

Johnson, Sylvia. *Mosses.* Minneapolis: Lerner Publishing, 1983.

Johnson, Sylvia. *Snakes.* Translated from Japanese. Minneapolis: Lerner Publishing, 1986.

Lavies, Bianca. *Compost Critters.* New York: Dutton's Children's Books, 1993.

MacQuitty, Miranda. *Discovering Foxes.* New York: The Bookwright Press, 1988.

Mell, Jan. *The Scorpion.* New York: Crestwood House (Macmillan), 1990.

Overbeck, Cynthia. *Ants.* Minneapolis: Lerner Publishing, 1982.

Pembleton, Seliesa. *The Pileated Woodpecker.* Minneapolis: Dillon Press, 1989.

Penny, Malcolm. *Discovering Beetles.* New York: The Bookwright Press, 1986.

Phillips, Roger. *Mushrooms.* Boston: Little, Brown and Co., 1991.

Preston-Mafhum, Ken. *Discovering Centipedes and Millipedes.* New York: The Bookwright Press, 1990.

Sherrow, Victoria. *The Porcupine.* Minneapolis: Dillon Press, 1991.

Index

Page numbers in *italics* refer to illustrations.

About the Author

Jo S. Kittinger finds creativity in nature. As a potter, freelance crafts designer, writer, and illustrator, she can take common clay and turn it into a vase, or a summer's breeze and turn it into a story. Her work has appeared in numerous books, magazines, and newspapers. *Dead Log Alive!* is her first children's book. She lives with her family and a menagerie of pets in Hoover, Alabama.